Cities and Statecraft
in the
Renaissance

LIZANN FLATT

 Crabtree Publishing Company

www.crabtreebooks.com

Renaissance World

Author: Lizann Flatt
Editor-in-Chief: Lionel Bender
Editor: Simon Adams
Project coordinator: Kathy Middleton
Photo research: Susannah Jayes
Design concept: Robert MacGregor
Designer: Ben White
Production coordinator: Ken Wright
Production: Kim Richardson
Prepress technician: Ken Wright

Consultant: Lisa Mullins, Department of History and
  Philosophy of Science, University of Cambridge

Cover photo: Pinturicchio, Bernardino (1454-1513)
  Enea Silvio Piccolomini crowned as a poet by Frederick III.
  Scene from the Life of Pius II.
  Location :Libreria Piccolomini, Duomo, Siena, Italy
  Photo Credit : Scala / Art Resource, NY

Photographs and reproductions:
The Granger Collection, NYC/TopFoto: pages 1, 5, 7, 8, 10,
  14, 18, 19, 20, 22, 23, 24, 25, 26, 27, 28, 29, 30
iStockphoto.com: pages 9, 17
Topfoto: pages 6 (©ullsteinbild), 11 (Topham/Picturepoint),
  12 (Spectrum/HIP), 13 (© Fiore), 16 (©Art Media/HIP),
  31 (©ullsteinbild)
Topham Picturepoint: page 4, 15, 21

Photo on page 1: Fresco by Amrogio Lorenzetti, 1337–40,
  showing the effects of good government

This book was produced for Crabtree Publishing Company
  by Bender Richardson White

Library and Archives Canada Cataloguing in Publication
Flatt, Lizann

  Cities and statecraft in the Renaissance / Lizann Flatt.
(Renaissance world) Includes index.
ISBN 978-0-7787-4595-2 (bound).--ISBN 978-0-7787-4615-7
(pbk.)

  1. Renaissance--Juvenile literature. 2. Cities and towns--
Europe--History--Juvenile literature. 3. City and town life--
Europe--History--Juvenile literature. 4. Europe--Commerce-
-History--Juvenile literature. 5. Europe--Civilization--
Juvenile literature. I. Title. II. Series: Renaissance world
(St. Catharines, Ont.)

CB361.F53 2010   j940.2'1   C2009-902427-6

Library of Congress Cataloging-in-Publication Data
Flatt, Lizann.

  Cities and statecraft in the Renaissance / Lizann Flatt.
    p. cm. -- (Renaissance world) Includes index.
  ISBN 978-0-7787-4615-7 (pbk. : alk. paper) --
  ISBN 978-0-7787-4595-2 (reinforced library binding : alk. paper)
  1. Renaissance--Juvenile literature. 2. Cities and towns--Europe--
History--Juvenile literature. 3. City and town life--Europe--History--
Juvenile literature. 4. Europe--Commerce--History--Juvenile litera-
ture. 5. Europe--Kings and rulers--History--Juvenile literature. 6.
Europe--Civilization--Juvenile literature. I. Title. II. Series.
  CB361.F55 2010
  940.2'1--dc22

                                        2009016726

Crabtree Publishing Company

www.crabtreebooks.com   1-800-387-7650
Copyright © **2010 CRABTREE PUBLISHING COMPANY**. All rights reserved. No part of this publication may be reproduced,
stored in a retrieval system or be transmitted in any form or by any means, electronic, mechanical, photocopying, recording, or otherwise,
without the prior written permission of Crabtree Publishing Company. In Canada: We acknowledge the financial support of the Government
of Canada through the Book Publishing Industry Development Program (BPIDP) for our publishing activities.

Published in Canada
Crabtree Publishing
616 Welland Ave.
St. Catharines, Ontario
L2M 5V6

Published in the United States
Crabtree Publishing
PMB16A
350 Fifth Ave., Suite 3308
New York, NY 10118

Published in the United Kingdom
Crabtree Publishing
White Cross Mills
High Town, Lancaster
LA1 4XS

Published in Australia
Crabtree Publishing
386 Mt. Alexander Rd.
Ascot Vale (Melbourne)
VIC 3032

Contents

The Renaissance   4

Trade   6

Italian City-States   8

Life in the City   12

Ideas and Individuals   14

Achievements in Architecture   16

Weapons and War   18

Monarchs Gain Might   20

Expanding the Empire   24

Rules for Rulers   26

Politics and Religion   28

Power and the People   30

Further Reading, Web Sites, Glossary, Index   32

The Renaissance

The European Renaissance began around 1300 and continued to the early 1600s. "Renaissance" means "rebirth" in French.

A Time of Change

During the Renaissance, scholars and artists looked back more than 1,000 years to rediscover the ideas of ancient Greece and Rome in art, literature, science, architecture, and politics. Italy was the first country to experience this rebirth. These ideas later spread to the rest of Europe. New lands were discovered, and the printing press was introduced, which helped spread new ideas. The discovery of gunpowder led to the creation of deadlier weapons. People began to realize that they had a say in how they were governed. It was a time of great change in the way people lived their lives, in the way they related to other countries, and in the way their governments were run.

The Renaissance began soon after the first deadly outbreak of **bubonic plague**. The plague was caused by a bacterium that is carried by rats. These rats had fleas. When a flea bit an infected rat, it carried the bacterium to other rats and to any humans it later bit. The plague caused fever, aching limbs, vomiting of blood, and swollen lymph glands in the neck, armpit, and groin. Lymph glands are also called buboes, which is where the name "bubonic plague" comes from. The disease also caused blackening of the skin, so the disease also came to be known as the Black Death.

The seaport of Venice was an important entry point for goods on their way for sale in other places in Europe, making Venice a wealthy city. By 1400 the city had about 3,000 boats in its fleet. Venice's contact with far-away regions not only brought it wealth, it also brought Venice into contact with the bubonic plague that arrived from Asia.

Spread of Sickness

The plague spread from Asia to Europe along **trade routes.** As **merchants** brought **trade** goods such as spices and cloth from the East to Italian cities, they also brought with them rats and people who were infected. The first outbreak of plague happened late in 1347 and lasted until about 1350. In that time the disease killed 20 to 30 million people, nearly one-third of Europe's population. Smaller outbreaks continued in Europe until 1700.

Effects of the Plague

Many people died from the plague, and the drop in population had a huge impact on the economy and how people lived. People who owed others money died and business was disrupted. Often there were not enough peasants left to work on rich lords' lands to harvest their crops. Those workers that survived demanded more money or better conditions for doing their jobs. Sometimes the lord and his entire family died, so the peasants moved to the city to look for work. Some city governments stopped working for a time as lawyers, judges, and rulers fell ill. Trade nearly stopped during the plague.

With death everywhere, some people thought they should enjoy their lives instead of working so hard. Others questioned why God had not stopped the plague, and lost their faith in the Church. Cities were hit hardest but recovered faster than rural areas as they offered more jobs and opportunities.

A person visiting a patient with the plague holds a sponge soaked with vinegar and spices to his nose because plague victims gave off a foul smell. Two attendants hold torches in an attempt to fumigate, or clean, the air.

TIMELINE

1337–1453 Hundred Years' War between England and France

1347–50: First outbreak of plague in Europe

1454: Italian city-states sign a truce with the Peace of Lodi

1494: France invades Italy

1519–21: Spanish conquest of the Aztec empire in Mexico

1555: Peace of Augsburg recognizes Protestantism

1580–1640: Spain occupies Portugal

1588: England defeats the Spanish Armada

1608: French explorer Samuel de Champlain sets up a trading post in present-day Quebec

1618–48: Thirty Years' War in the Holy Roman Empire involves most of Europe

1642–60: Civil war and upheaval in England

1648: Spain gives official independence to the Dutch Republic of the United Provinces, or the Netherlands

Trade

The growth of trade gave cities an increased importance in Renaissance society. Urban areas increased in size and a new group of people who had money emerged. These new rich people wanted a say in how their cities were governed.

Urbanization

Along the main roads used for trade, towns sprang up at stopping places for people on their journeys. Increased trade brought more people to these urban areas as merchants, craftworkers, and shopkeepers arrived to make and sell their goods. People began to move into the cities from the surrounding countryside. Some wanted to escape a life of poverty as a peasant. Increased trade and commercial activity meant more jobs in workshops, factories, and shipyards, as well as the possibility of training as an artist, architect, or craftworker.

Noble families moved into a city to mingle with other nobility and rich merchants. When towns were small the people could govern themselves in a loose arrangement called a commune. As a town grew into a city, it needed more rules and ways to govern those who lived there. Cities needed people to enforce rules, collect taxes, and do other important jobs.

Changing Money

Different regions used different types of money, or currency, so moneychangers became necessary. A merchant could go to a moneychanger and trade one currency for another in order to do business in a different region. These moneychangers began to accumulate a lot of money, and so did merchants when they made profits. With lots of money, these people became bankers.

City financial departments, such as this one in Siena in 1493, had to keep track of what taxes people owed and how much tax people paid. Taxes are how a city raises money from its citizens to perform services of government, such as making and enforcing laws and keeping its citizens safe from attack.

Merchant Banking

Bankers lent money for a fee to merchants—even nobles, princes, and kings—and made more money when the businesses they had helped establish were successful. Merchants did not want to carry around large numbers of coins so they gave their money to a banker to keep it safe. Bankers charged a small fee to do this. Often, if a noble could not pay back a loan, some of their land had to be given to the banker as payment for the loan. In this way bankers and merchants grew rich and, with this money, gained power. They demanded more say in city government to make sure that no laws or taxes were put into place that were unfair to their interests.

More Money

Even people who lived in rural areas were affected by trade with cities. Rural people could sell their agricultural products to a nearby city. They were paid with money, not by payment in kind with other goods or services, as was done in the Middle Ages. Nobles or landowners also began to want payment in money from their tenants or serfs instead of payment in labor or agricultural products. The nobles wanted to use money to buy things such as cloth or jewels that merchants and craftworkers were selling.

The End of Feudalism

Society in the **Middle Ages** was organized in a system called feudalism. This meant that a landholding lord gave nobles, called vassals, land in exchange for their sworn loyalty, support, and services in times of war. The land given to a vassal was called a fief.

The Church also owned fiefs. A vassal did not own his fief, but he could manage the peasants on it, collect taxes from them, and give out justice. When he died his son usually inherited the fief and provided the same services to the lord as his father had done. When trade put more money into use, feudalism began to crumble. A soldier could be paid with money, not land. Cities became richer and more important, were better able to defend themselves. They had less need for a lord who often lived far away.

The harbor at Genoa, on the Mediterranean Sea, made it an important trading port and naval power. Genoa fought Venice for control of the trade routes to the East but was defeated in 1380, and Venice gained control.

Money enabled Italian cities to become independent of their landowning nobles. Smaller cities joined with, or were overtaken by, larger cities or regions until five main regions existed. These regions fought each other for territory and trade.

Guilds

Merchants and craftworkers in the cities banded together in groups called **guilds**. There were guilds for stonemasons, carpenters, **apothecaries**, silkmakers, and many other professions. This allowed them to control what price they bought and sold things for and how much they paid their workers. Members of the merchant and banking guilds became very wealthy. They wanted more power in government to have a say in matters that directly affected them, such as taxes, and to be sure that justice was equal between nobles and non-nobles.

Guilds to Governments

The local noble families often fought vendettas with each other. These were long-standing feuds that required a family to preserve its honor by avenging a family member's death or insult. But one family

avenging a death required that the other family must then get revenge as well. This led to ongoing problems, especially when nobles now lived close together in a city and were no longer separated by distance as they had been in the country. People, and many nobles, wanted peace and order in the city.

The desire for peace often led one powerful leader, a *signori*, to seize power. These powerful men had a loyal following and brought peace to the city. The less wealthy, such as laborers, were not allowed to form guilds and were generally excluded from government because guild membership was often a requirement for government. Their exclusion later become a source of conflict.

Lorenzo de' Medici took over the leadership of Florence from his father in 1469 and ruled until his death. Known as "the Magnificent," he was a great patron of the arts.

Taxes

A city needs money to pay for its lawyers, judges, accountants, and numerous other government workers. A wealthy city can also afford to pay soldiers to defend it from attack. To get money, a city collects taxes. Taxes are money a government demands from its citizens in exchange for providing government services. Italian cities charged taxes on property people owned, on the sale of goods within a city, and when goods were moved into and out of the city. This money allowed a city to function independently of a noble upon whose land it might originally have been established.

Regions and Rivalries

A region dominated by a city and including the surrounding countryside is called a **city-state.** Florence, Venice, and Milan were considered city-states. These three together with the Kingdom of Sicily and the Papal States made up the five main regions in Italy at the height of the Renaissance. They had differences in their forms of government, but the one common element was that they all had a strong central government dominated by a single powerful person who had emerged to lead the state.

Italian Embassies

Italian governments established embassies, or buildings, in other Italian states in which their ambassadors lived to observe the activities of that state. The ambassadors sent back reports to their home state. The idea that an embassy in another country is actually part of its own home state's territory arose from this practice, as within the embassy, people only had to follow the laws of their embassy's home country.

The city of Bologna had many towers built by rich noble families who competed with one another to show off their wealth. Bologna was a prosperous city. Its university was an important school of law from as early as 1100.

Rulers

Milan was ruled by dukes, Naples had kings, and the Papal States were ruled by the pope, the head of the Roman Catholic Church. The Republic of Venice had a form of elected government but its membership was limited to certain families. The leader and most prestigious person was the Doge, an elected position given for life. The character of the leader had a huge impact on the city. Many rulers commissioned or paid for the creation of new buildings, paintings, sculptures, and churches. In this way they contributed to the artistic achievements of the Renaissance.

Republic of Florence

The city-state of Florence is considered the birthplace of the Renaissance. It was an important banking center for all Europe.

The government in Florence was organized as a **republic** and governed by a council called the Committee of the Priors, made up of nine men. Eight of these men were elected by members of the 21 guilds. Those eight men then chose a ninth man to be the *gonfalonier* of justice, or head of the council.

In reality, the wealthy Medici banking family controlled Florence for many years, as different family members often held high government positions. With so much money made from banking, the family could bribe or give money to councilors in exchange for favors, and use loans or donations to reward or punish supporters or enemies. Under the Medicis, the florin, or gold coin, of Florence became the standard coin used throughout Europe.

Arrival of the Ambassadors *by Vittore Carpaccio. An ambassador's job was to negotiate agreements between governments. Ambassadors could enter and leave a country when they wanted to, and the local state's laws could not prevent them from doing their jobs, which might have involved spying.*

Diplomacy

Powerful states that existed so close together in Italy established a new way of relating to each other. Diplomacy is the use of discussions and negotiations by rulers or by their professional **diplomats**. Diplomacy does not include force such as war but it can include the threat of war. Its purpose is to strengthen the state without going to the expense and upheaval of war. The state gets something it wants without antagonizing the other state it is negotiating with.

Italian states sent representatives on diplomatic missions. If a ruler went to another state, it caused too much attention and was highly risky, for the ruler could be killed or captured while away. Sending a representative instead became common. At first they might go for three months to two years. As states became larger and wars more frequent, regular diplomacy became necessary, so it made sense to establish a permanent envoy or **ambassador.** Members of the wealthy merchant classes or young sons of nobles were given jobs as diplomats and ambassadors. Once diplomats were living in another state for a longer period, hosting social functions became important. They employed their own cooking staff to help with the entertaining and to ensure the diplomat was not poisoned. Italian states began to send diplomats to other politically powerful countries, such as France, and the practice of Italian diplomacy soon spread.

Cesare Borgia used force to take over parts of central Italy and deceived and killed his enemies to maintain his power. He was the model for the ideal, cunning ruler in Niccolo Machiavelli's book The Prince.

Balance of Power

No one Italian region could dominate all the others because the remaining states aligned themselves to fight against it. This is called a balance of power. The situation was formalized with the Peace of Lodi, a treaty signed in 1454 to end a war between Milan and Venice. Their allies also had to accept this peace. But the peace did not last. Conflicts arose, and the regions were so used to fighting each other that they could not unite against the invasions by other European monarchies that began in 1494.

Life in the City

Life in a Renaissance city was busy and bustling with activity. Cities held exuberant carnivals and festivities to celebrate their heritage and their beautiful surroundings. Citizens developed a real sense of civic pride.

Celebrations

Cities held festivals on Church holy days but also as important celebrations of civic pride, or pride about the greatness of a city. The cities competed against each other for how grand their celebrations were. These events usually included a special **mass** or church service, parades, feasts, fireworks displays, horse races, mock battles, poetry contests, and religious dramas.

Venice's most important festival was the Marriage with the Sea, a 15-day event on the anniversary of Venice's rescue of the country of Dalmatia from the control of pirates. It also took in the celebration of Ascension Day. The Doge first went to mass, then led a parade of boats out to sea. He blessed the water and dropped a gold ring overboard as a sign of respect or homage to the sea.

In the spring, Florence celebrated the Feast of San Giovanni (Saint John the Baptist). Before the festival, balconies lining the parade route were draped with cloth. The entire piazza, or main town square, was covered with a canopy. Merchants displayed valuable goods such as jewels, armor, or reliquaries (ornate containers for religious artifacts) to honor the city. The parade of floats showing scenes from the Bible made its way through the city two days before the feast. The day before the feast, members of the clergy wearing embroidered clothes of gold and silks paraded through town, beginning and ending at the cathedral. A fireworks display was held at night. On June 24 there was a special mass and then a horse race.

A modern horse race in Siena, the Palio delle contrade, *first held in 1482. Horse races were part of many Renaissance festivals. In Siena, horses and riders race three times around the main square for the palio or silk banner.*

Carnivals

Cities also held carnivals just before Lent, the 40-day religious period leading up to Easter when people went without things such as meat. Carnivals were lavish festivals of excess involving feasts, wearing masks and other disguises, singing and dancing, and playing jokes. It was a time when the rich and the poor mingled together freely in the streets, ignoring the usual social rules that kept them separate the other days of the year.

City Sections

Cities were organized in neighborhoods or quarters. In the center of the city was the piazza. The city's cathedral would be nearby, as were the main buildings such as the town hall, where the government officials met. People who worked at the same occupation often lived near one another. Jews often lived in a separate section. In 1516 Jews in Venice were forced to live on the site of an old iron foundry where iron was worked. The two entrances were gated and manned by soldiers at night and in the morning. The word "ghetto" is thought to come from the old Venetian word *getto*, meaning foundry.

Living in a Palazzo

An Italian noble or rich merchant lived in a palazzo or townhouse arranged around an interior courtyard. The street level floor was used for the merchant's business, with the family and servant living quarters on the upper floors. The kitchen was upstairs so

The site of the Jewish ghetto in Venice still exits today, although it is now a pleasant, mixed neighborhood. All Jews in Venice were once forced to live here.

Villas

In addition to their townhouses, wealthy families often owned a villa, a large house with lots of land in the country. They lived at their villas in the summer to escape the heat and crowds of the city. Laborers worked on the land, growing crops such as grapes, grain, olives, and fruits.

smoke would not flow through the house. A palazzo had a grand salon or room for family entertaining, a private chapel, a dining room, and bedrooms with joining rooms where toilets emptied down chutes.

Ideas and Individuals

A humanist education was the ideal training for Renaissance leaders, princes, and royalty, but education also became more accessible for more citizens.

Humanism

Humanism is the name given to the Renaissance idea that humans and the human experience are important and worth

A portrait by Titian of Isabella d'Este. Isabella's father believed in the equality of women so she was educated. She was one of the first people to buy artwork because of who the artist was rather than because of the artwork's subject.

studying. With trade routes opening up and providing more contact with the Middle East, European scholars discovered the wealth of learning that went on there. They searched out ancient **manuscripts** and read these original texts, not just the later writings about them. They found new information about history, medicine, philosophy, and more. Humanism stressed the study of grammar, argument, history, poetry, and morality. It brought education outside **monasteries** and into schools and homes. Humanists believed that the main reason for education was to teach people to become well-rounded, knowledgeable citizens.

Who Learned?

As in earlier days, kings, princes, and nobles received an education. Rich merchants hired humanists to educate their children so that they would have the skills needed to carry on their business. Counting, record keeping, and reading contracts became important skills for a merchant.

Italian schools educated boys from wealthy families in their own cities but many schools came to accept gifted boys from all over, no matter what their economic situation was. Girls were not allowed to go to school, but those from a wealthy family were educated at home by tutors. Most working-class and rural children received little education.

Language

Education in the Renaissance was given in **Latin,** the language of ancient Rome, which limited participation to churchmen and scholars. Leon Battista Alberti, a prominent architect, wrote *On the Family* (1435-44) about methods of education. He suggested that the natural place for education was in the home, not in an institution, and stressed the important role fathers play in educating their children. He wrote in Italian, because he believed education was so important it should be available to all.

Subjects Taught

A humanist education stressed a variety of subjects. Students were taught not only religion, as in the past, but also mathematics, music, poetry, painting, **rhetoric,** athletics,

and military skills. Once educated, it was expected that these students would live an active life using their education to help their city or country and their fellow citizens. Those who came to Italy for an education took humanist ideas back with them to their own country. This helped spread Renaissance ideas in painting, sculpture, architecture, and government to other parts of Europe. The ideal humanist education was designed to prepare a man to meet any situation and handle it with ease and confidence.

This painting shows the hill of knowledge that represents the ideal humanist education. Students begin at the gates of grammar and then move to the levels of math, logic, music, astronomy, geometry, rhetoric, and theology.

Father of Humanism

Petrarch, born Francesco Petrarca in 1304, is called the "father of humanism" because he discovered and preserved many classical manuscripts. He was more interested in the way these manuscripts expressed things than in what they actually said. He applied this style to his own writings. His collection of poems expressed intense personal feelings, which was a new approach at the time. His poetry became a model for the sonnet, a form of verse with 14 lines and a fixed rhyming scheme. Petrarch also believed that Italy should unite to carry on the goals of ancient Rome.

Achievements in Architecture

In Renaissance cities a new, organized style of architecture developed. Many new buildings were built in this style and new types of buildings came into being.

Style

In the Middle Ages buildings were tall because walls enclosed their towns, so the only available space in which to build was up. But as Renaissance cities expanded, they often got rid of their walls, so buildings could now spread sideways. Renaissance style is based on domes, columns, and arches borrowed from classical Greece and Rome. Rows of windows or arches gave buildings an organized appearance. A distant element, perhaps a door or the altar of a church, was framed behind an arch or row of columns.

Cathedrals

The cathedral was an essential building for any Renaissance city, and many cathedrals were built all over Europe during this period. Architect Filippo Brunelleschi completed the building of the Florence cathedral by adding its dome. This was the greatest architectural accomplishment of the time, as the dome capped a space 138 feet (42 meters) across. Brunelleschi had studied the classical buildings of ancient Rome and was able to build the dome without the massive temporary structures and supports that the standard building techniques would have required. The Florence cathedral was a great source of civic pride. It was a symbol of power for the city and for the wool guild that helped pay for it.

This painting shows the view of an ideal Renaissance city. It has wide boulevards and main buildings facing a large open piazza. The open spaces were as important to the overall design as the buildings themselves.

St. Peter's basilica in Rome is the largest church in the world and is considered to be the crowning achievement of construction during the Renaissance. It took about 160 years to build spanning the reigns of 22 popes. The central portion or nave is 600 feet (183 meters) long while the inner dome soars 370 feet (112 meters) high. Famous architects Donato Bramante, Raphael, and Michelangelo were among those involved. It was officially consecrated or blessed on November 18, 1626.

New Buildings

Architects were no longer employed just by the Church. Princes, merchants, and bankers now made use of an architect's skills, demanding buildings that were used for new and different purposes. Wealthy men had new palazzos, or townhouses, built for themselves, as well as new villas, or country residences. The printing press made books available to many more people. Libraries were built to house these books. The Church built a new library in Rome because its collection of manuscripts and books had outgrown the original building. New schools were built all over Europe. Theaters too were built as plays became more popular.

As an outward sign of their goodness, wealthy people or guilds commissioned the building of almshouses for the poor and foundling homes for orphans. Hospitals were also built, many of them attached to a convent because nuns ran them. As they were designed to show the link between religion and medicine, they were often built in the shape of a cross with a chapel in the center so that sick people could go to mass.

As the Renaissance style spread to the rest of Europe, it was modified into a national style. The palace of Versailles was planned as the palatial home of the French king.

City Planning

Architects began to plan civic buildings and spaces as a whole rather than as individual elements. They designed one main building to hold all the different government offices rather than have them scattered all over the city. Long, wide, straight streets replaced the narrow winding streets of medieval cities. Main buildings were grouped around a central piazza, the focal point for a city that was filled with fountains and statues.

Renaissance leaders often went to war to solve their differences. New weapons and types of soldiers, and the introduction of gunpowder, all revolutionized warfare.

Hand Weapons

Early in the Renaissance two types of bow were used. The crossbow, mounted horizontally on a wood frame, used a trigger to fire a bolt-like arrow. The longbow, which was about as tall as a man with an arrow half as long, was held vertically. The crossbow took longer to load and fire than a longbow but required less skill to use. Crossbows were effective at short to medium range while a longbowman could accurately shoot six arrows a minute at an enemy 200 to 500 yards (180–450 meters) away. Arrows from both bows could penetrate a knight's chainmail, an armor made of fine links of chain. As a result, knights began wearing armor in thicker, smooth plates. A halberd was like an ax with a hook on the back of the head. At close range, soldiers used it to pierce a knight's suit of armor or to pull him off his horse. The pike was a long hardwood pole up to 12 feet (3.7 meters) long with a sharp point. Soldiers used pikes to fend off mounted knights.

Gunpowder

The discovery of gunpowder, a black powder that explodes when it comes in contact with heat, changed war the most. Gunpowder was invented in China in the 900s and arrived in Europe around 1200. Exploding gunpowder creates hot gas and smoke. If the gas is kept in a tight space with an open end, it will force an object out of that opening.

The Renaissance painter Leonardo da Vinci also designed weapons of war for his patrons. Here is one of his design sketches for military machines done between 1487 and 1490.

New Weapons

A cannon, using gunpowder to fire stones or metal balls, could break through a city's protective stone wall. Grenades, or bombs that could be thrown, were also invented. Special units of powerful soldiers called grenadiers specialized in throwing them at targets. No longer did a high wall around a city provide protection from enemy troops.

The arquebus and then the musket, both early rifles, came into use as improvements were made to their trigger mechanisms. A bullet could penetrate a suit of armor so thicker plates of armor were needed. This increased its weight, so partial armor came into use. Soon only the breastplate and helmet were worn.

Warriors

Italian city-states hired paid soldiers, called mercenaries, to fight instead of relying on its own militia of male citizens because a city could lose many of them if the militia fought in battle. As ever-larger armies were needed, city-states hired a *condottiere* or contractor and drew up an agreement with him to produce several thousand soldiers for war. Rulers began to fear that these *condottieri* might take over the state, since they had the troops to do so. They started to negotiate with non-Italian warriors from countries such as Germany and England. Under contract, a military captain agreed to serve a single city-state. If he did not, he could be fined, or fired, or even executed.

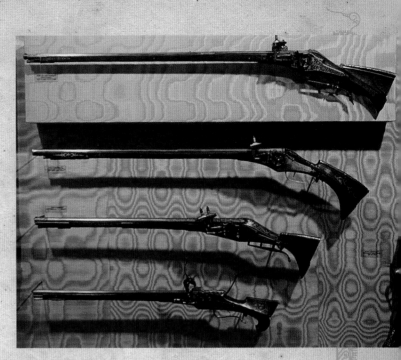

Guns such as these from Italy, Germany, and Portugal replaced bows and arrows on the battlefield in the mid to late 1500s.

Mercy and Mercenaries

When cities hired mercenaries as required, many of them were not willing to fight very hard in case they seriously wounded their opponents. They might be fighting against someone they'd gotten to know well while on the same side in a previous fight. Or they could end up on the same side as the current opponent in the next war.

States rewarded loyal captains, often giving them land and noble status. This helped to prevent captains from serving other rulers, although sometimes a ruler would make some extra money by hiring out his army to help other friendly states. In this way armies gradually came under the permanent employment of one state.

Monarchs Gain Might

While the Italian city-states and regions fought one another, European monarchs started to unite their own countries, creating larger areas ruled by one king.

Monarchy

A monarchy is a form of government where the authority to rule is given to a single king or emperor who reigns as long as he or she lives. This right to rule is usually passed down from father to son. Members of the king's family were called the royal family.

This scene of Louis XI of France with his court was painted in the 1400s. Known as "The Spider," Louis could be a cruel ruler, but he also built roads and canals, encouraged learning, and helped industry and agriculture.

A prince or son who was in line to inherit a throne was referred to as the crown prince, or the dauphin in France.

In ancient times and the early Middle Ages, a king was a landholding noble who was elected by other nobles to lead them in war. During times of peace he had little power over the nobles and ruled mostly over his own personal lands. The nobles that elected the king would sometimes form a council to advise him on government affairs. This council was the origin of parliament in England and the estates-general in France. Different monarchs agreed to give this council more or less power depending on their style of rule.

In England, Edward I opened up the advisory council with leading nobles and heads of the church in 1295. Together they formed a model parliament with knights from different regions, town representatives, and less important church leaders. In 1297, Edward agreed not to collect certain kinds of taxes without consulting this parliament. France's estates-general consisted of representatives from three estates or groups of people. They were the nobles, clergy, and common people. The estates-general first met in 1302 but then met occasionally, when the king needed to raise more money. They did not have the power to make laws.

England and France

In northern Europe, England and France fought each other on and off from 1337 to 1453, a war known misleadingly as the Hundred Years' War. The war began when Edward III of England claimed the French crown. The fighting weakened both countries and caused their kings to turn their attention away from each other and towards gathering power at home for themselves. In England, Henry Tudor defeated his rival, Richard III, in battle in 1485. He become King Henry VII. He gained further support from his enemies by marrying his rival's niece. Henry worked closely with parliament and kept England out of wars in Europe. He also cut the power of the nobility by appointing people to jobs based on their ability and loyalty to himself and not on their noble rank or position.

After the Hundred Years' War, the French king, Louis XI, was determined to gain control of the nobles. Charles the Bold, Duke of Burgundy, was one of his main rivals and wanted his territories to remain independent of France. When Charles tried to take over a town in northeastern France, he was killed in the battle and Louis took over most of his lands. In 1481 he added three more regions, giving him control of most of France.

Henry VII, king of England from 1485 to 1509, established the Star Chamber, a court used to put powerful nobles on trial. Like most courts of the time, it used torture to get confessions.

Claims to the Throne

Sometimes a monarch would die with no male heir to the throne. This often led to power struggles and even war as other branches of the family claimed the right to rule. If a monarch died and his heir was still a child, another family member would rule for the child as a regent. A regent might not always want to give up the throne when the child heir became an adult, and war could break out as his allies fought the allies of the royal child.

The Holy Roman Empire

At the start of the Renaissance most people in Europe were Christians. This meant they followed the teachings of the Roman Catholic Church, whose leader is the pope. The pope was responsible for all matters relating to the spirituality of the people. Responsibility for the secular or worldly matters of the people fell to the Holy Roman Emperor. His **empire** was centered in what is now Germany but also included parts of present-day France, Italy, the Netherlands, Belgium, Switzerland, Austria, and the Czech Republic. It contained many different princedoms, dukedoms, church lands, and city-states. The emperor was elected by the nobles and other leaders of the empire but crowned and approved by the pope and Church officials. In 1438 Albert II became emperor, bringing the Austrian Habsburg family to the throne. The Habsburgs brought in a military system, courts, and a law-making body of government.

Spain

In the late Middle Ages, Spain consisted of three main Christian kingdoms and one region controlled by Muslims, people who practice the religion of Islam. In 1469, a marriage between the prince of Aragon and the princess of Castile ended rivalries between their two kingdoms. They later became king and queen of Spain and brought much of the country under their joint control. In 1492, they led an army to conquer the Muslims in Granada in the south, forcing them to **convert** to Christianity or leave Spain. In 1512, they took over the remaining kingdom of Navarre, uniting Spain for the first time.

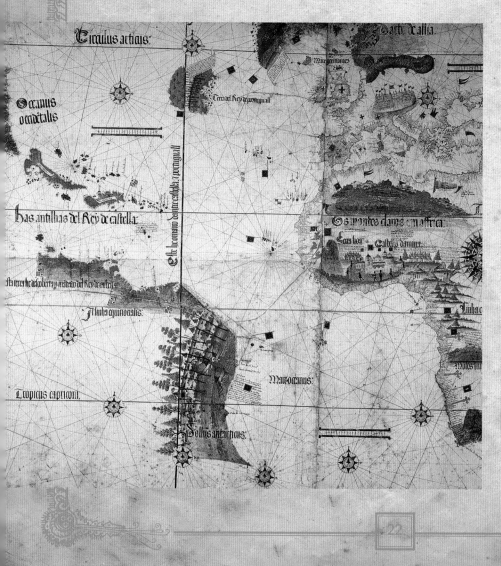

A world map from 1502 showing the boundary line that ran down the middle of Brazil and divided the world between Spain and Portugal.

Portugal

In 1385, John I became king of Portugal. He defended Portugal against its neighbor, Spain, and formed an alliance with England. The Portuguese fishermen and traders had gained a lot of knowledge about the ocean and built ships that were capable of making long voyages. Sponsored by his son Henry, known as "the Navigator," Portuguese sailors began to explore the coast of Africa and eventually sailed to India, making their country rich through exploration and trade.

Monarchy and Marriage

The royal families of Europe used marriage to create alliances with one another. England's Henry VII arranged for his son Arthur to marry Catherine of Aragon, daughter of Spain's king and queen. When Arthur died, Henry VII arranged for her to marry his second son Henry. Maximilian I, Holy Roman Emperor from 1493 to 1519, married his son Philip to Joanna, another daughter of the Spanish monarchs. These alliances related most royal families to one another but also led to rival claims to a throne once the children of these marriages became old enough to rule.

King Ferdinand and Queen Isabella of Spain used the excuse that Muslim-run Granada refused to pay dues to Spain, to invade and conquer the country in 1492. They wanted to unite Spain as a Christian nation. The Muslims surrendered and then left the country or converted to Christianity.

Dividing Line

In 1492, Spanish monarchs, Ferdinand and Isabella, sponsored Christopher Columbus's discovery of new lands across the Atlantic Ocean. This created conflict between Spain and Portugal because the two nations were involved in overseas exploration. Pope Alexander VI announced in 1493 that the world would be divided between the two countries either side of a line running down the middle of the Atlantic. Spain received the Americas to the west and Portugal received Africa and India to the east. In 1494, the two countries agreed on their own treaty at Tordesillas in Spain that moved that line to the west, giving Brazil to Portugal. The treaty did not stop other nations from exploring and claiming these lands, with Spain and Portugal losing land to the Netherlands, England, and France.

With more power in their own countries, European monarchs looked to gain more wealth, power, and political influence by discovering or conquering other parts of the world to build up their own empires.

Italy Invaded

King Charles VIII of France marched with his army into Florence in 1494. Initially helped by the Duke of Milan to further his interests against the Kingdom of Naples, Charles moved on towards his own goal of taking over Naples. But an alliance between Spain, the Holy Roman Empire, Milan (which had changed its mind after seeing the powerful French army), and Venice forced him to retreat. He returned to France greatly influenced by the Renaissance ideas he was exposed to. By 1521, the new kings of France and Spain were fighting over Italy. By 1559, almost all of Italy was under Spanish rule.

Exploration

Both Spain and Portugal paid for early voyages of exploration. Italian explorer Christopher Columbus landed in the Bahamas under the Spanish flag in 1492. Vasco da Gama sailed around the tip of Africa to reach India in 1498, allowing Portugal to set up trading partnerships in the East. These voyages meant items such as spices, jewels, and silks were brought back and sold to other European merchants for large profits. Seeing the wealth that these discoveries had brought Spain and Portugal, England, France, and the Netherlands began to sponsor their own explorations. John Cabot, Henry Hudson, and Jacques Cartier claimed land in North America, establishing lucrative fur, cod, and whaling industries. These discoveries helped these nations expand their wealth and influence.

This engraving shows Sir Francis Drake's ship attacking a Spanish treasure ship off the coast of South America in 1579. England's Elizabeth I encouraged such acts of piracy, giving Drake ships and money for his voyages in return for a share of the captured treasure.

New World Conquests

Spanish knights who had no land sailed to the New World in search of land from which to earn an income. Known as conquistadors, or conquerors, they overwhelmed the peoples they came into contact with. The Spanish brought weapons, such as steel swords and guns, and warhorses that the peoples of the Americas had never seen before. They also brought contagious diseases such as smallpox, which killed thousands of native people.

The Spanish conquistador Hernán Cortés met a native woman who knew the Mayan and Aztec languages. Using her as an interpreter, he persuaded some of the Mayan Indians to fight with him against the Aztecs. The Aztec emperor Montezuma II ruled millions of people. His capital city, Tenochtitlán, was built on an island in the middle of Lake Texcoco. At the time the Spanish arrived, there were 200,000 people living in the city and surrounding lands. After the Spanish defeated the Aztecs, they rebuilt the city with Spanish-style buildings and renamed it Mexico City.

Spanish conquistador Francisco Pizarro took over the capital of the Inca empire in South America in 1533. The Incas had just ended a civil war so their forces were weakened. Pizarro captured the emperor and killed many nobles. Spanish soldiers were given land and the Incas who survived were forced to work as slaves mining gold and silver.

A scene showing Chesapeake harbor and a tobacco warehouse, taken from the map of Virginia, one of England's American colonies. During the Renaissance, tobacco trading became an important industry.

New World Achievements

The Aztecs had developed a 365-day solar calendar. The Incas were skilled farmers, making use of terraces and canals to irrigate the land and made use of natural fertilizers, such as bird droppings, to improve their crops. Foods such as chilies, chocolate, corn, potatoes, squash, pumkin, coconuts, and pineapples were brought to Europe from the New World.

Fur Trade

In North America, French explorers began to trade metal items such as fishhooks, knives, and pots, as well as other goods, with the native peoples in exchange for beaver pelts, or skins with fur. The pelts were in great demand in Europe, where they were made into fashionable felt hats.

As European rulers fought to gain power over one another, thinkers of the day published new theories on the rights, duties, and responsibilities of a princely ruler or government.

The cover image from Thomas More's description of an ideal society he called "Utopia." The book's title is derived from Greek words that mean "no where." Even today the word "utopian" refers to an unattainable or unrealistic goal.

Ends Justify the Means

Niccolo Machiavelli was an Italian statesman who went on diplomatic missions on behalf of Florence. These missions involved negotiations with France, Germany, and the pope, and included a journey to spy on Cesare Borgia, son of Pope Alexander VI, who was attempting to establish his own princedom that would include Florence. Through his experiences and observations as a government official and diplomat, and his study of history, Machiavelli came to view politics in a new way.

Machiavelli's views were published in *The Prince* in 1532. He thought of the state as a living thing with the ruler or prince as its head and the people as its body. His belief was that a healthy state was unified, orderly, and balanced and that its people would then have honor, happiness, security, and strength. But he also believed that an unhealthy state was disorderly and that the ruler could and should do anything necessary to preserve the state and restore its healthy balance. Machiavelli believed it was justifiable to do this even if it meant the ruler had to do things that were deceptive or cruel and that the use of force was acceptable. *The Prince* has influenced many leaders and political thinkers. Even today, if something is described as being Machiavellian, it means it is cruel and cunning.

An Ideal State

Thomas More began his career in law and in 1518 he was employed as a royal councilor and ambassador for Henry VIII. He wrote his most famous work *Utopia* in 1516 in Latin. In it he wrote about his belief in an ideal society in which the government ensured there was justice and equality for everyone. He also set out the ideal economic and social conditions of that society.

More had an idealistic and Christian attitude towards government. This led him to criticize the state of national government in his time. More refused to swear an oath agreeing that Henry VIII ranked above all rulers, even the pope. He was convicted of treason, or crimes against the state, and beheaded in 1535.

Above the Rules

Jean Bodin, an expert in French law, wrote the *Six Books of the Republic* in 1576. In it he argued that kings had the right to rule over their subjects but were not bound by the civil laws that ordinary people had to obey. He wrote that kings had supreme power over the state. He did believe that rulers should be constrained by social customs and the laws of nature under God. His theory was used as the cornerstone of the belief in the Divine Right of Kings. Late Renaissance kings used this to justify their belief that they could rule as they liked because they been given the right to rule by God directly.

Frescoes by Ambrogio Lorenzetti, painted in 1337–39, line three walls in the room where Siena's government officials met. They show the effects on the town and countryside of both good and bad government.

Father of International Law

Hugo Grotius, a Dutch lawyer, theologian, and statesman, spent the end of his career as Swedish ambassador to France. He published *On the Law of War and Peace* in 1625. This expressed for the first time the idea that all nations should follow certain rules of behavior. His work was used to settle wars and make treaties and is the foundation of the belief that all countries should follow the same code of law.

Wars in Renaissance Europe were mainly about the control of land and political power, but many were also based on religious beliefs.

Protestant Reformation

The Reformation began in 1517 when Martin Luther, a German monk, protested some of the practices and teachings of the Catholic Church. Luther's demands for Church reform gathered support. His followers, or Protestants, refused to pay their tithes to the Church. Other Protestant movements began, notably John Calvin's Presbysterian Church in Geneva. As Protestantism gained strength, the Church became alarmed at the loss of revenue and the challenge to its authority. Catholic rulers persecuted Protestants. Protestants wanted the right to practice their own religion and, when they were in power, persecuted Catholics.

Internal Religious Conflicts

After the Reformation, many Protestants in France followed the teachings of John Calvin. Called Huguenots, they were persecuted by the Catholic-dominated government. Civil war broke out between the two in the 1560s. When the Catholic king died without an heir, the next in line for the throne, Henry, was a Huguenot. Catholic soldiers prevented him from entering Paris so Henry converted to Catholicism, giving a limited religious freedom to Huguenots.

England broke with the Catholic Church when Henry VIII failed to get the Pope to annul, or cancel, his marriage. Henry declared himself head of the English Church instead of the pope and forced the nation to change its religion. His successor, Edward VI, was a Protestant and his successor, Mary I, a Catholic. When Elizabeth I became queen in 1558, she established a Protestant Church.

This miniature shows the power of the Holy Roman Empire under Charles V. Charles ruled not just the empire but also Spain as well.

Spanish Armada

In 1588 Spain organized a fleet of ships called the Spanish Armada with which to invade England and return the country to Catholicism. But as the Armada began its attack, the Dutch prevented some of the Spanish troops stationed in the Netherlands from meeting and boarding their ships.

Freedom of Religion

Many people who disagreed with the accepted religion of their home country, or who were persecuted for their religious beliefs, were forced to leave their homeland. Puritans, who wanted reforms in the Anglican Church, left England in 1620 on board the *Mayflower* and sailed for America. Huguenots or French Protestants left Catholic France for the Americas, the Netherlands, and England. In 1654 the first Jewish people to arrive in America settled in what is now New York City.

At sea, the English filled eight ships with gunpowder, set them on fire, and sent them towards the Spanish fleet. The English defeat of the Armada was a great victory, symbolizing both England's naval power and also its resistance to Catholicism.

Holy Roman Empire

The Holy Roman Empire was involved in two different religious wars. To its east, the empire was threatened by the growing power of the Muslim Ottoman Empire. Internally, the Holy Roman Empire was divided by the Protestant Reformation. Peasants and the lower classes hoped the Reformation would free them of economic obligations to the Church and the nobles who controlled them. In 1524–26, the peasants revolted, but were crushed by the nobles. Then, in 1546, the emperor and the Catholic princes went to war against a group of Protestant princes. Peace was achieved in 1555 when Lutheran churches were legally allowed to exist in the Empire.

The defeat of the Spanish Armada, a fleet of about 130 warships, in 1588 by English ships was an especially important victory because Protestant England feared a forced return to Catholicism if it was defeated by Catholic Spain.

During the Renaissance people began to protest when they didn't agree with how they were governed. Strong rulers still held power, but the idea of basic rights of freedom of religion and good government had taken hold among the people.

Early Protests

The Jacquerie in 1358 was a revolt in northern France. Rebelling against harsh social conditions, the peasants attacked castles and killed nobles. The nobility squashed their efforts violently. In Florence, laborers staged the Ciompi Rebellion of 1378 to gain a voice in government. Three new guilds were created that represented them in the republic's government, although the rich merchants regained control after three years. In England, the Peasants' Revolt of 1381 was a reaction in part against a poll tax, money

each individual had to pay the state regardless of their income. This meant the tax was much harder for the peasants to pay than for the rich. While these protests did not have a lasting impact on governments, they proved that people could take action.

State Rules Over Religion

The Thirty Years' War between 1618–48 was a series of conflicts involving the Holy Roman Empire and neighboring states. Protestants and Catholics continued to disagree over the 1555 Peace of Augsburg that was meant to solve their differences. That agreement also dissatisfied those Protestant groups, such as the Calvinists, who were left out. The loss of lives and the destruction of property during the war rendered the empire powerless, and its power soon passed to local princes that determined their own religion.

French Catholics demonstrate against the coronation of the Protestant Henry IV. He soon converted to Roman Catholicism and in 1598 put into effect the first long-lasting act of religious tolerance, the Edict of Nantes. This granted Protestants the right to practice their own religion.

The French Monarchy

France emerged from the Thirty Years' War with more land and more power. Louis XIV believed in the Divine Right of Kings, which stated that God had given him power to rule and he was accountable only to God. Louis was his own chief minister, working directly with other ministers to run the country. He built the luxurious palace of Versailles and made his nobles live there so he could keep an eye on them and prevent them from organizing any uprisings against his rule. France would not overthrow its monarchy until 1789, when revolution broke out.

The English Parliament

Elizabeth I of England gave parliament more power than some of the previous monarchs. She used parliament to raise taxes and introduce laws so that its members would support her government. Parliament was not happy when her successor, James I, took away some of its privileges.

In 1628, in the early years of the reign of his son Charles I, parliament drew up the Petition of Right, in which it said a monarch was not allowed to introduce taxes without parliament's permission and could not put people in jail without just cause. Charles tried to rule without parliament but ran out of money and was forced to recall it in 1640. Civil war between king and parliament erupted in 1642 and from 1649 England briefly had a republican government before the monarchy was restored in 1660.

Rights take Root

American settlers who had come from England believed that they should have the same rights in the American colonies as they had had in England. Rights such as a trial by jury and the right to not be imprisoned without just cause were among the most important. They also believed an accused person had the right to have legal help at trial. Wanting to write down these and other rights that they had followed through the centuries in England, and adding in rights concerned with life in America, they created the U.S. Constitution.

Catholic and Protestant armies battle in June 1619 during the Thirty Years' War. The dispute was over the Protestants' right to practice their religion that was being taken away by the new Catholic emperor.

Further Reading and Web Sites

Quigley, Mary. *The Renaissance.* Heinemann, 2003
Cole, Alison. *Eyewitness: Renaissance.* Dorling Kindersley, 2000
Morley, Jacqueline. *A Renaissance Town.* New York: Peter Bedrick, 2001
Mason, Antony. *Everyday Life in Renaissance Times.* Minnesota: Smart Apple Media, 2006

Teacher Oz's Kingdom of History—Renaissance: www.teacheroz.com/renaissance.htm
Renaissance Personalities: www.yesnet.yk.ca/schools/projects/renaissance/
Renaissance Connection: www.renaissanconnection.org

Glossary

ambassador High-ranking diplomat of a country sent to another country as a permanent representative

apothecary Someone who provides medicines or remedies

bubonic plague Deadly disease caused by a bacterium that is carried by rats; also known as the Black Death

city-state Region dominated by a city

convert Change; to turn someone from one religion to another

diplomat Professional negotiator or messenger sent by the ruler of one country to the leader of another to discuss matters of common concern

empire A large group of states or countries under the control of one emperor and government

guild Organization with a membership of all the people employed in the same profession, craft, or skill

Latin The language used in ancient Rome

manuscript Book or other document written by hand

mass, the Roman Catholic church service in which bread and wine are consecrated or blessed to represent the body and blood of Christ

Merchant A person who buys, sells, and trades in goods, often with another country

Middle Ages Period of European history from about AD 400 to the Renaissance, also known as medieval times

monastery Place where monks or nuns live to follow religious rules

republic A country governed by an elected ruler, not one who inherited the throne, such as a monarch

rhetoric The art of using speech or writing to persuade or influence someone

trade The business of buying and selling goods

trade route A road or sea passage along which trade is conducted between two countries or cities

Index

Americas, the 25, 31
architecture 16, 17
armies 19
banking 7, 10
Bodin, Jean 27
bubonic plague 4, 5
cathedrals 16
cities 6, 8, 13, 17
city-states 9, 10, 19, 20
diplomacy 11
education 14, 15
embassies 9
England 20, 21, 23, 25, 28, 29, 30, 31
exploration 24, 25
festivals 12, 13
feudalism 7
Florence 10, 12, 24, 30

France 20, 21, 24, 26, 28, 30, 31
fur trade 25
government 4, 8, 9, 10, 30
Grotius, Hugo 27
guilds 8
gunpowder 18
Holy Roman Empire 22, 23, 28, 29, 30
houses 13
humanism 14, 15
languages 15
Machiavelli, Niccolo 26
Medici family 8, 10
mercenaries 19
merchants 6, 7
monarchy 20, 21, 23

money 6, 7, 10
More, Thomas 26, 27
Petrarch 15
Portugal 23, 24
Reformation 28
religion 28, 29, 30, 31
Renaissance, definition of 4
Spain 22, 23, 24, 29
Spanish Armada 29
taxes 9
Tordesillas, treaty of 22, 23
trade 5, 6, 7, 24, 25
Venice 4, 9, 10, 11, 12, 13
weapons 18, 19

Printed in China — CT